Do It Yourself

Holiday Craft

Do It Yourself

Holiday Craft

Author
Vinnie Mathur

Illustrator/ Design
Himani Pundir

Graphic Designer
Bhupender Singh

Galgotia Publications pvt. ltd.

Second Edition 2010

ISBN:- 81-7515-589-2

Published by Suneel Galgotia for Galgotia Publications Pvt. Ltd.,
5, Ansari Road, Darya Ganj, New Delhi-110 002 and
printed at :- Tara Art Printers Pvt. Ltd.

Galgotia Publications pvt. ltd.

CONTENTS

Diwali

Diya Decoration

Decorate plain diyas with your creativity...

1

Take an ordinary plain wax diya from the market.

Things required

Plain ceramic wax diya

Sliver or golden ceramic paint

Sparkles

Fevicol

Gota, laces, sequins etc.

2

Paint it in any colour of your choice. You can also use different sparkle tubes to put all around the diya to decorate it.

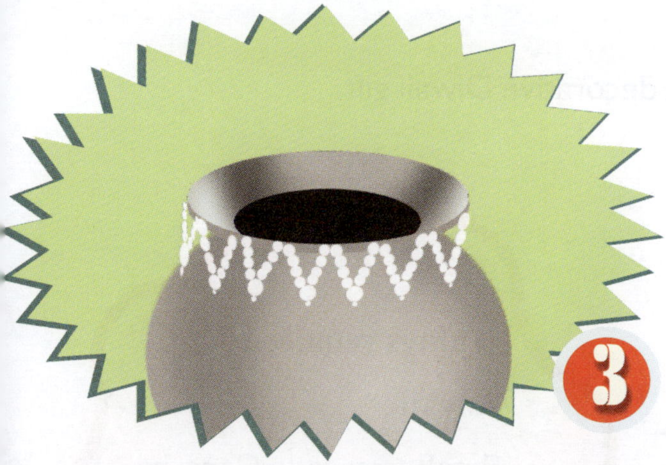

Further decorate it by covering the diya with gota or lace. Decorate many more diyas like this and celebrate Diwali with great pomp and show.

Such diyas will highly compliment your diwali decoration.

Ganesha On Tile

Convert this ordinary tile into a decorative Diwali gift...

Take any old tile lying at home and paint it with any colour of your choice.

Things required

Any tile

Small terracotta Ganesha idol

Fevicol

Sparkles

Dry flowers

Golden paint

Paints & Brushes

Make a nice border with golden colour paint.

3

Take some dried flowers from the market and stick on the left side of the tile. Now take Ganesha idol and stick on top right corner of the tile. You can also attach a diya or agarbatti stand on it.

Your Ganesha tile is now ready.

Ganesha Coaster

Convert ordinary glass coasters to decorative ones...

Take an old wedding card and trace the Ganesha from the card on to the coaster with the help of black liner.

Things required

Glass paints of any three colours

Black glass liner

Old wedding card

Glass coaster

Once the liner has dried, take glass paints and colour the picture.

3

Let it dry for a day and your coaster is ready.

Make many more like these to gift to your near and dear ones.

Christmas
Pop up Card

Send Xmas greetings to your friends by making this pop up card...

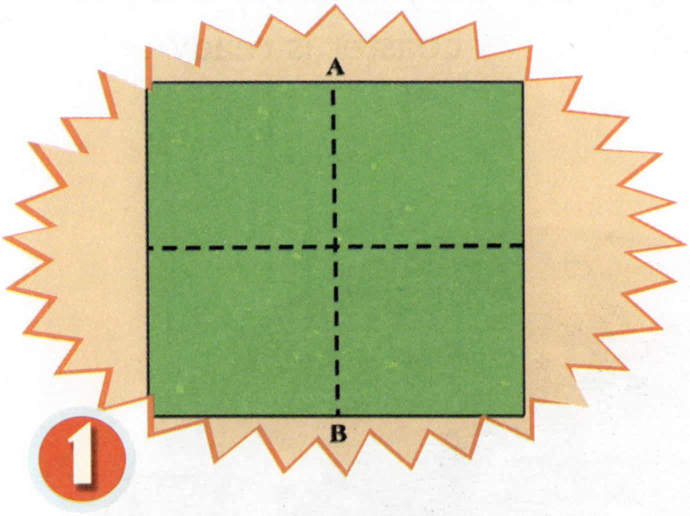

Things required

Piece of card-16 x10 cms.

Pencil

Colour

Scissors

Fold card in half, along line A to B.

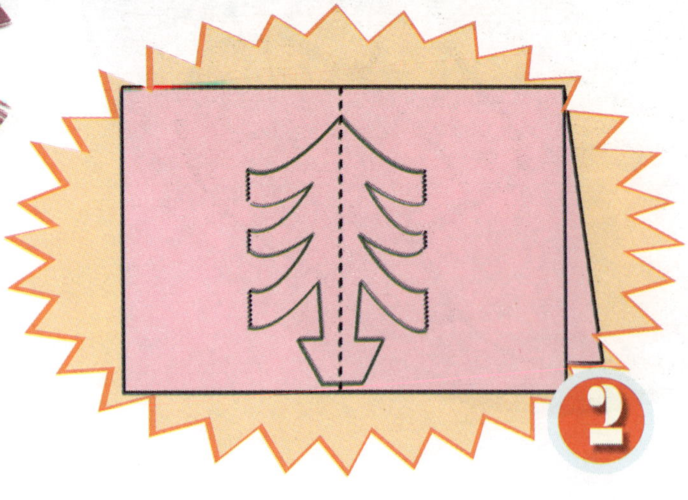

Draw a christmas tree in the centre of the card. Cut along red line, but leave the ends of branches uncut.

3

Push christmas tree towards you, and fold the centre crease the other way. Now close the card.

4

colour and decorate the tree. Write 'Merry Christmas' and a lovely message for your friend.

Xmas is celebrated every year on 25th December all around the world.

Xmas Cracker

Make a Xmas Cracker for your friends on Xmas...

Things required

2 Empty ice cream cups

Kitchen foil or gift paper

Scissors

Crafty glue

Toffees or gifts

Red or green ribbon

Cellotape

Cut the paper and flatten it. Take one ice-cream cup and put a gift or some toffees in it.

Cover the first cup with the second mouth to mouth.

Holding the cups tightly, wrap cellotape and the gifted paper around them.

Tie coloured ribbons to grip the paper close to the ends of the cups so that your cracker is firm.

Cut the end of the papers with scissors. You can also use mistle toe, holly, stars etc for decorating it further.

Eid
Greeting Card

Take a piece of card and cut it into a round shape.

Things required

Piece of card

Sketch pens

Glitter

Fevicol

Sparkles

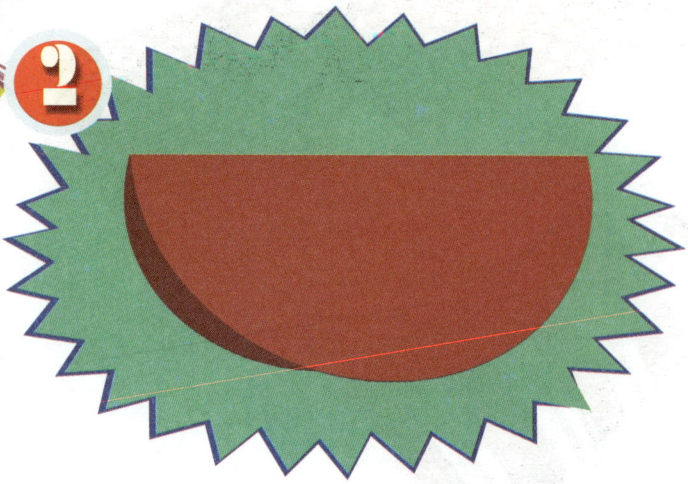

Now fold it into half in the shape of a half moon.

Now decorate the card with sparkles and write 'Happy Eid' on it with sketch pens. Also sprinkle some glitter on the card.

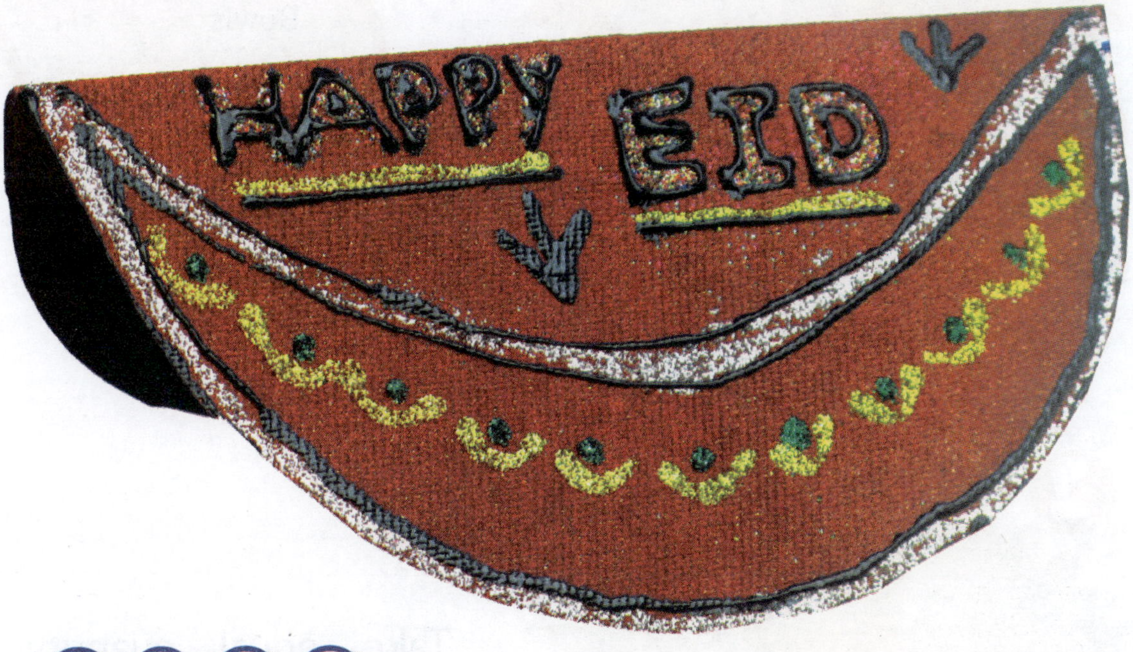

Your attractive Eid card is now ready. Eid Mubarak!

Holi

Glittering Green

Organic and herbal colours are safe to use, so let us make four lovely colours at home...

Things required

Flour

Mehndi powder

Bowls

Spoons

1

Take a packet of mehndi powder and some flour from the kitchen and put them in two different bowls.

2

Take equal quantity of mehndi powder and flour and mix them together.

Mix both the powders well. Now your green colour is ready.

Sunny Yellow

Things required

Besan

Haldi

Flour

Bowls

Spoons

Take equal quantity of besan and haldi in two different bowls.

Now mix haldi and besan well.

3

To increase the quantity, add some flour to it. Now your yellow colour is ready.

Scintilating Red

Things required

- Red hibiscus flowers' powder
- Sandal powder (chandan)
- Flour
- Bowl
- Spoon

1

Dry red hibiscus flowers in shade and then grind them to make powder.

2

Now take equal quantity of hibiscus flowers' powder and sandal powder in a bowl and mix them well.

3

To increase the quantity, you can also mix some flour in the same amount.

4

Hibiscus flowers' powder and chandan powder have a beautiful red colour which is extremely beneficial for the skin. This can be used instead of red gulal.

Easter
Easter Eggs

Let us eggs for Easter! decoration

Take one broken egg, clean it and put toffees in one of the broken part.

Things required

Eggs

Toffees

Brush

Paints

Sparkle Tube

Cellotape

Now tape the two parts of the broken egg together with cellotape.

Paint the outer part of the egg with different colours of your choice.

Further decorate with sparkles and gift to your friends. Happy Easter !

Mother's Day
Jewellery Box

This box will surely prove as the best gift for your mom...

1

Take any old cookie tin and clean it from inside.

Things Required

- Any old round cookie box
- Fevicol
- Decorative material like old rakhis, laces etc.
- Old colourful dupatta
- Acrylic paints

2

Paint the cookie tin with acrylic colours of your choice or paste any red colour cloth or old dupatta all around it neatly.

For decoration, you can stick bindis, stars, sequins, mirror etc in a fancy manner all around the box.

Use sparkles to further enhance it. Put some goodies for mummy and add a note 'I love you mummy' and gift her on Mother's Day.

Father's day

Desk Tider

Make this lovely desk tider for your father and present him on Father's Day...

Take a small sweet box or a paint box and cover it with ice-cream sticks from all four sides.

Things Required

A small square old paint box or a sweet box

Few ice-cream sticks

Fevicol

Sparkles

Ribbon

Keep the back side of the box longer by stretching the cover of the box straight as shown in the picture. Now the frame of the desk tider is ready.

Decorate the desk tider by using ribbon flowers and paste it on one side of the frame. Mirrors, old rakhis, laces can also be used to further enhance the beauty. Your Father's Day gift is ready.

Father's Day is celebrated every year in the month of June.

Grandparents' Day
Gift Box

Let us learn the technique of glass painting and make this gift box for your grandparents...

1

Take an empty gift box which has a plain glass top.

Things required

Any 3 or 4 fevicryl glass paints

Black glass liner

Empty glass top box

Any design of your choice

Old newspaper

Oil pin

2

Choose any design of your choice like a Ganesha design from an old diwali greeting card.

Place the design under the glass top and outline it with black liner.

Let it dry and then fill in the design with colours of your choice. If you see bubbles appearing while using colours, prick them immediately with an oil pin.

5

Again let it dry for a few hours. Your gift box is ready to be filled in with cookies for your grandparents.

Your Ganesha gift box is now ready to be gifted.

Rakshabandhan
Decorative Rakhi

Your brother will definitely get impressed with this Rakhi made with love and affection...

Things required

Kalava

Scissors, fevicol

Old copy cover

Sparkles

Paints

Brushes

1

Take an old copy cover or any piece of cardboard, cut it into a star shape and paint it with any poster colour. Let it dry.

2

After it dries, decorate it with sparkles.

You can decorate it by putting mirrors on the border also.

Now glue this to a kalava thread and your Rakhi is ready.

Rakshabandhan is the pious festival of brothers and sisters.

Janmashtmi

Flute

Play this lovely flute on Janmashtmi and impress everyone...

Things required

Flute

Stars and sequins

Sparkles

Fevicol

Acrylic paints or wool

Take an ordinary flute from the market and cover it with coloured wool.

Alternately you can paint it with any colour of your choice.

Decorate it with mirrors, sequins etc. You can also use sparkles on it to decorate it further. Now your lovely flute is ready to play.

Make such flutes for your friends and cousins.

Teacher's Day
Satin Diary Cover

Impress your teacher with this beautiful diary...

Things required

Any old colourful piece of cloth

Sparkles

Fevicol

Scissors

1

Take any diary and cut the cloth piece according to its size.

2

Turn piece of cloth upside down and place the diary on it. Now put fevicol on the cloth and stick it on the diary cover.

Wrap sides and bottom of the cloth around the edge of the diary.

Decorate the cover with sparkles or fabric paints.

Dr. Radhakrishnan's birthday is celebrated as Teacher's Day on 5th sept. every year.